LINCOLN'S LAST HOURS

LINCOLN'S LAST HOURS

BY
CHARLES A. LEALE, M.D.

KALPAZ

ISBN: 978-93-5128-689-9(HB)

First Published in 1909
Indian Reprint in 2017

Published by

Kalpaz Publications
C-30, Satyawati Nagar,
Delhi – 110052
E-mail: kalpaz@hotmail.com
Website: kalpazpublications.com
Ph.: +91-9212142040

Lincoln's Last Hours

By Charles A. Leale, M. D.

Commander and Companions of the Military Order of the Loyal Legion of the United States:

At the historic pageant in Washington, when the remains of President Lincoln were being taken from the White House to the Capitol, a carriage immediately preceding the catafalque was assigned to me. Outside were the crowds, the martial music, but inside the carriage I was plunged in deep self-communion, until aroused by a gentle tap at the window of my carriage door. An officer of high rank put his head inside and exclaimed: "Dr. Leale, I would rather have done what you did to prolong the life of the President than to have accomplished my duties during the entire war." I shrank back at what he said, and for the first time realized the importance of it all. As soon as I returned to my private office in the hospital, I drew down the window-shade, locked the door, threw myself prostrate on the bare wood floor and asked for advice. The answer came as distinctly as if spoken by a human being present: "Forget it all." I visited our Surgeon General, Joseph K. Barnes, and asked his advice; he also said: "Cast it from your memory."

On April 17, 1865, a New York newspaper reporter called at my army tent. I invited him in, and expressed my desire to forget all the recent sad events, and to occupy my mind with the exacting present and plans for the future.

Recently, several of our Companions expressed the conviction, that history now demands, and that it is my duty to give the detailed facts of President Lincoln's death as I know them, and in compliance with their request, I this evening for the first time will read a paper on the subject.

Lincoln's Last Hours

One of the most cruel wars in the history of the world had nearly closed.

The people of the United States were rejoicing at the prospect of peace and returning happiness. President Lincoln, after the surrender of General Robert E. Lee, visited Richmond, Virginia, exposing himself to great danger, and on his return delivered an address from the balcony of the White House.

I was then a Commissioned Officer in the Medical Department of the United States Army, having been appointed from my native State, New York, and was on duty as Surgeon in charge of the Wounded Commissioned Officers' Ward at the United States Army General Hospital, Armory Square, Washington, District of Columbia, where my professional duties were of the greatest importance and required constant and arduous attention. For a brief relief and a few moments in the fresh air I started one evening for a short walk on Pennsylvania Avenue. There were crowds walking toward the President's residence. These I followed and arrived just at the commencement of President Lincoln's last public address to his people. From where I stood I could distinctly hear every word he uttered and I was profoundly impressed with his divine appearance as he stood in the rays of light, which penetrated the windows of the White House.

The influence thus produced gave me an intense desire again to behold his face and study the characteristics of the "Savior of his Country." Therefore on the evening of April 14, 1865, after the completion of my daily hospital duties, I told my Ward Master that I would be absent for a short time. As a very large number from the Army stationed near Washington frequently visited the city, a general order was in force that none should be there without a special pass and all wearing uniform and out at night were subject to frequent challenge. To avoid this inconvenience officers stationed in Washington generally removed all signs of their calling when off duty. I changed to civilian's dress and hurried to Ford's Theatre, where I had been told President Lincoln, General Grant, and Members of the Cabinet were to be present to see the play, "Our American Cousin." I arrived late at the theatre, 8.15 p. m., and requested a seat in the orchestra, whence I could view the occupants of the President's box, which on looking into the theatre, I saw had been beautifully decorated with American flags in honor of the occasion. As the building was crowded the last place vacant was in the dress circle. I was greatly disappointed, but accepted this seat, which was near the front on the same side and about 40 feet from the President's box, and soon became interested in the pleasing play.

Suddenly there was a cheering welcome, the acting ceased temporarily out of respect to the entering Presidential party. Many in the audience rose to their feet in enthusiasm and vociferously cheered, while looking around. Turning, I saw in the aisle a few feet behind me, President Lincoln, Mrs. Lincoln, Major Rathbone and Miss Harris. Mrs. Lincoln smiled very happily in acknowledgment of the loyal greeting, gracefully curtsied several times and seemed to be overflowing with good cheer and thankfulness. I had the best opportunity to distinctly see the full face of the President, as the light shone directly upon him. After he had walked a few feet he stopped for a moment, looked upon the people he loved and acknowledged their salutations with a solemn bow. His face was perfectly stoical, his deep set eyes gave him a pathetically sad appearance. The audience seemed to be enthusiastically cheerful, but he alone looked peculiarly sorrowful, as he slowly walked with bowed head and drooping shoulders toward the box. I was looking at him as he took his last walk. The memory of that scene has never been effaced. The party was preceded by a special usher, who opened the door of the box, stood to one side, and after all had entered closed the door and took a seat outside, where he could guard the entrance to the box. The play was resumed and my attention was concentrated on the stage until I heard a disturbance at the door of the President's box. With many others I looked in that direction, and saw a man endeavoring to persuade the reluctant usher to admit him. At last he succeeded in gaining an entrance, after which the door was closed and the usher resumed his place.

For a few moments all was quiet, and the play again held my attention until, suddenly, the report of a pistol was heard, and a short time after I saw a man in mid-air leaping from the President's box to the stage, brandishing in his hand a drawn dagger. His spur caught in the American flag festooned in front of the box, causing him to stumble when he struck the stage, and he fell on his hands and knees. He quickly regained the erect posture and hopped across the stage, flourishing his dagger, clearing the stage before him and dragging the foot of the leg, which was subsequently found to be broken, he disappeared behind the scene on the opposite side of the stage. Then followed cries that the President had been murdered, interspersed with cries of "Kill the murderer!" "Shoot him!" etc., from different parts of the building. The lights had been turned down, a general gloom was over all, and the panic-stricken audience were rushing toward the doors for exit and safety.

I instantly arose and in response to cries for help and for a surgeon, I crossed the aisle and vaulted over the seats in a direct line to the President's box, forcing my way through the excited crowd. The door of the box had been securely fastened on the inside to prevent anyone following the assassin before he had accomplished his cruel object and made his escape. The obstruction was with difficulty removed and I was the first to be admitted to the box.

The usher having been told that I was an army surgeon, had lifted up his arm and had permitted me alone to enter.

I passed in, not in the slightest degree knowing what I had to encounter. At this moment, while in self-communion, the military command: "Halt!" came to me, and in obedience to it I stood still in the box, having a full view of the four other occupants. Then came the advice: "Be calm!" and with the calmest deliberation and force of will I brought all my senses to their greatest activity and walked forward to my duty.

Major Rathbone had bravely fought the assassin; his arm had been severely wounded and was bleeding. He came to me holding his wounded arm in the hand of the other, beseeching me to attend to his wound. I placed my hand under his chin, looking into his eyes an almost instantaneous glance revealed the fact that he was in no immediate danger, and in response to appeals from Mrs. Lincoln and Miss Harris, who were standing by the high-backed armchair in which President Lincoln sat, I went immediately to their assistance, saying I was a United States army surgeon. I grasped Mrs. Lincoln's outstretched hand in mine, while she cried piteously to me, "Oh, Doctor! Is he dead? Can he recover? Will you take charge of him? Do what you can for him. Oh, my dear husband!" etc., etc. I soothingly answered that we would do all that possibly could be done. While approaching the President, I asked a gentleman, who was at the door of the box, to procure some brandy and another to get some water.

As I looked at the President, he appeared to be dead. His eyes were closed and his head had fallen forward. He was being held upright in his chair by Mrs. Lincoln, who was weeping bitterly. From his crouched down sitting posture it was evident that Mrs. Lincoln had instantly sprung to his aid after he had been wounded and had kept him from tumbling to the floor. By Mrs. Lincoln's courage, strength and energy the President was maintained in this upright position during all the time that elapsed while Major Rathbone had bravely fought the assassin and removed the obstruction from the door of the box.

I placed my finger on the President's right radial pulse but could perceive no movement of the artery. For the purpose of reviving him, if possible, we removed him from his chair to a recumbent position on the floor of the box, and as I held his head and shoulders while doing this, my hand came in contact with a clot of blood near his left shoulder. Remembering the flashing dagger in the hand of the assassin, and the severely bleeding wound of Major Rathbone, I supposed the President had been stabbed, and while kneeling on the floor over his head, with my eyes continuously watching the President's face, I asked a gentleman to cut the coat and shirt open from the neck to the elbow to enable me, if possible, to check the hemorrhage that I thought might take place from the subclavian artery or some other blood vessel. This was done with a dirk knife, but no wound was found there. I lifted his eyelids and saw evidence of a brain injury. I quickly passed the separated fingers of both hands through his blood matted hair to examine his head, and I discovered his mortal wound. The President had been shot in the back part of the head, behind the left ear. I easily removed the obstructing clot of blood from the wound, and this relieved the pressure on the brain.

The assassin of President Lincoln had evidently carefully planned to shoot to produce instant death, as the wound he made was situated within two inches of the physiological point of selection, when instant death is desired. A Derringer pistol had been used, which had sent a large round ball on its awful mission through one of the thickest, hardest parts of the skull and into the brain. The history of surgery fails to record a recovery from such a fearful wound and I have never seen or heard of any other person with such a wound, and injury to the sinus of the brain and to the brain itself, who lived even for an hour.

As the President did not then revive, I thought of the other mode of death, apnoea, and assumed my preferred position to revive by artificial respiration. I knelt on the floor over the President, with a knee on each side of his pelvis and facing him. I leaned forward, opened his mouth and introduced two extended fingers of my right hand as far back as possible, and by pressing the base of his paralyzed tongue downward and outward, opened his larynx and made a free passage for air to enter the lungs. I placed an assistant at each of his arms to manipulate them in order to expand his thorax, then slowly to press the arms down by the side of the body, while I pressed the diaphragm upward: methods which caused air to be drawn in and forced out of his lungs.

During the intermissions I also with the strong thumb and fingers of my right hand by intermittent sliding pressure under and beneath the ribs, stimulated the apex of the heart, and resorted to several other physiological methods. We repeated these motions a number of times before signs of recovery from the profound shock were attained; then a feeble action of the heart and irregular breathing followed.

The effects of the shock were still manifest by such great prostration, that I was fearful of any extra agitation of the President's body, and became convinced that something more must be done to retain life. I leaned forcibly forward directly over his body, thorax to thorax, face to face, and several times drew in a long breath, then forcibly breathed directly into his mouth and nostrils, which expanded his lungs and improved his respirations. After waiting a moment I placed my ear over his thorax and found the action of the heart improving. I arose to the erect kneeling posture, then watched for a short time, and saw that the President could continue independent breathing and that instant death would not occur.

I then pronounced my diagnosis and prognosis: "His wound is mortal; it is impossible for him to recover." This message was telegraphed all over the country.

When the brandy and water arrived, I very slowly poured a small quantity into the President's mouth, this was swallowed and retained.

Many looked on during these earnest efforts to revive the President, but not once did any one suggest a word or in any way interfere with my actions. Mrs. Lincoln had thrown the burden on me and sat nearby looking on.

In the dimly lighted box of the theatre, so beautifully decorated with American flags, a scene of historic importance was being enacted. On the carpeted floor lay prostrate the President of the United States. His long, outstretched, athletic body of six feet four inches appeared unusually heroic. His bleeding head rested on my white linen handkerchief. His clothing was arranged as nicely as possible. He was irregularly breathing, his heart was feebly beating, his face was pale and in solemn repose, his eyelids were closed, his countenance made him appear to be in prayerful communion with the Universal God he always loved. I looked down upon him and waited for the next inspiration, which soon came: "Remove to safety." From the time Mrs. Lincoln had placed the President in my charge, I had not permitted my attention to be diverted. Again I was asked the nature of his wound and replied in these exact words: "His wound is mortal; it is impossible for him to recover."

While I was kneeling over the President on the floor Dr. Charles S. Taft and Dr. Albert F. A. King had come and offered to render any assistance. I expressed the desire to have the President taken, as soon as he had gained sufficient strength, to the nearest house on the opposite side of the street. I was asked by several if he could not be taken to the White House, but I responded that if that were attempted the President would die long before we reached there. While we were waiting for Mr. Lincoln to gain strength Laura Keene, who had been taking part in the play, appealed to me to allow her to hold the President's head. I granted this request and she sat on the floor of the box and held his head on her lap.

We decided that the President could now be moved from the possibility of danger in the theatre to a house where we might place him on a bed in safety. To assist in this duty I assigned Dr. Taft to carry his right shoulder, Dr. King to carry his left shoulder and detailed a sufficient number of others, whose names I have never discovered, to assist in carrying the body, while I carried his head, going first. We reached the door of the box and saw the long passage leading to the exit crowded with people. I called out twice: "Guards, clear the passage! Guards, clear the passage!" A free space was quickly cleared by an officer and protected by a line of soldiers in the position of present arms with swords, pistols and bayonets. When we reached the stairs, I turned so that those holding the President's feet would descend first. At the door of the theatre, I was again asked if the President could be taken to the White House. I answered: "No, the President would die on the way."

The crowd in the street completely obstructed the doorway and a captain, whose services proved invaluable all through the night, came to me, saying: "Surgeon, give me your commands and I will see that they are obeyed." I asked him to clear a passage to the nearest house opposite. He had on side arms and drew his sword. With the sword and word of command he cleared the way. We slowly crossed the street. It was necessary to stop several times to give me the opportunity to remove the clot of blood from the opening to the wound. A barrier of men had been formed to keep back the crowds on each side of an open space leading to the house. Those who went ahead reported that the house directly opposite the theatre was closed. I saw a man standing at the door of Mr. Petersen's house, diagonally opposite, holding a lighted candle in his hand and beckoning us to enter. This we did, not having been interrupted in the slightest by the throngs in the street, but a number of the excited populace followed us into the house.

The great difficulty of retaining life during this brief time occupied in moving the President from the theatre to Mr. Petersen's house, conclusively proved that the President would have died in the street if I had granted the request to take him such a long distance as to the White House. I asked for the best room and we soon had the President placed in bed. He was lifted to the longitudinal center of the bed and placed on his back. While holding his face upward and keeping his head from rolling to either side, I looked at his elevated knees caused by his great height. This uncomfortable position grieved me and I ordered the foot of the bed to be removed. Dr. Taft and Dr. King reported that it was a fixture. Then I requested that it be broken off; as I found this could not satisfactorily be done, I had the President placed diagonally on the bed and called for extra pillows, and with them formed a gentle inclined plane on which to rest his head and shoulders. His position was then one of repose.

The room soon filled with anxious people. I called the officer and asked him to open a window and order all except the medical gentlemen and friends to leave the room. After we had given the President a short rest I decided to make a thorough physical examination, as I wished to see if he had been wounded in any other part of the body. I requested all except the surgeons to leave the room. The Captain reported that my order had been carried out with the exception of Mrs. Lincoln, to whom he said he did not like to speak. I addressed Mrs. Lincoln, explaining my desire, and she immediately left the room. I examined the President's entire body from his head to his feet and found no other injury. His lower extremities were very cold and I sent the Hospital Steward, who had been of great assistance to us in removing the President from the theatre, to procure bottles of hot water and hot blankets, which were applied. I also sent for a large sinapism and in a short time one very nicely made was brought. This I applied over the solar-plexus and to the anterior surface of his body. We arranged the bed clothes nicely and I assigned Dr. Taft and Dr. King to keep his head upon the pillows in the most comfortable position, relieving each other in this duty, after which I sent an officer to notify Mrs. Lincoln that she might return to her husband; she came in and sat on a chair placed for her at the head of the bed.

As the symptoms indicated renewed brain compression, I again cleared the opening of clotted blood and pushed forward the button of bone, which acted as a valve, permitted an oozing of blood and relieved pressure on the brain. I again saw good results from this action.

After doing all that was professionally necessary, I stood aside for a general view and to think what to do next. While thus watching several army officers anxiously asked if they could in any way assist. I told them my greatest desire then was to send messengers to the White House for the President's son, Captain Robert T. Lincoln, also for the Surgeon General, Joseph K. Barnes, Surgeon D. Willard Bliss, in charge of Armory Square General Hospital, the President's family physician, Dr. Robert K. Stone, and to each member of the President's Cabinet. All these desires of mine were fulfilled.

Having been taught in early youth to pay great respect to all religious denominations in regard to their rules concerning the sick or dying, it became my duty as surgeon in charge of the dying President to summon a clergyman to his bedside. Therefore after inquiring and being informed that the Rev. Dr. Gurley was Mrs. Lincoln's pastor, I immediately sent for him.

Then I sent the Hospital Steward for a Nelaton probe. No drug or medicine in any form was administered to the President, but the artificial heat and mustard plaster that I had applied warmed his cold body and stimulated his nerves. Only a few were at any time admitted to the room by the officer, whom I had stationed at the door, and at all times I had maintained perfect discipline and order.

While we were watching and letting Nature do her part, Dr. Taft came to me with brandy and water and asked permission to give some to the President. I objected, stating as my reason that it would produce strangulation. Dr. Taft left the room, and again came to me stating that it was the opinion of others also that it might do good. I replied: "I will grant the request, if you will please at first try by pouring only a very small quantity into the President's mouth." This Dr. Taft very carefully did, the liquid ran into the President's larynx producing laryngeal obstruction and unpleasant symptoms, which took me about half a minute to overcome, but no lasting harm was done. My physiological and practical experiences had led to correct conclusions.

On the arrival of Dr. Robert K. Stone, who had been the President's family physician during his residence in Washington, I was presented to him as the one who had been in charge since the President was shot. I described the wound and told him all that had been done. He said he approved of my treatment.

Surgeon General Joseph K. Barnes' long delay in arriving was due to his going first to the White House, where he expected to find the assassinated President, then to the residence of Secretary Seward and his son, both of whom he found requiring immediate attention, as they had been severely wounded by the attempts of another assassin to kill them.

On the arrival of the Surgeon General and Assistant Surgeon General, Charles H. Crane, I reported what we had done and officially detailed to the Surgeon General my diagnosis, stating that whenever the clot was allowed to form over the opening to the wound the President's breathing became greatly embarrassed. The Surgeon General approved the treatment and my original plan of treatment was continued in every respect until the President's death.

The Hospital Steward arrived with the Nelaton probe and an examination was made by the Surgeon General and myself, who introduced the probe to a distance of about two and a half inches, where it came in contact with a foreign substance, which lay across the track of the ball; this was easily passed and the probe was introduced several inches further where it again touched a hard substance at first supposed to be the ball, but as the white porcelain bulb of the probe on its withdrawal did not indicate the mark of lead it was generally thought to be another piece of loose bone. The probe was introduced the second time and the ball was supposed to be distinctly felt. After this second exploration nothing further was done with the wound except to keep the opening free from coagula, which, if allowed to form and remain for a short time, produced signs of increased compression, the breathing becoming profoundly stertorous and intermittent, the pulse more feeble and irregular. After I had resigned my charge all that was professionally done for the President was to repeat occasionally my original expedient of relieving the brain pressure by freeing the opening to the wound and to count the pulse and respirations. The President's position on the bed remained exactly as I had first placed him with the assistance of Dr. Taft and Dr. King.

Captain Robert T. Lincoln came and remained with his father and mother, bravely sustaining himself during the course of the night.

On that awful memorable night the great War Secretary, the Honorable Edwin M. Stanton, one of the most imposing figures of the nineteenth century, promptly arrived and recognized at that critical period of our country's history the necessity of a head to our Government and as the President was passing away established a branch of his War Department in an adjoining room. There he sat, surrounded by his counsellors and messengers, pen in hand, writing to General Dix and others. He was soon in communication with many in authority and with the Government and army officials. By Secretary Stanton's wonderful ability and power in action, he undoubtedly controlled millions of excited people. He was then the Master, and in reality Acting President of the United States.

During the night Mrs. Lincoln came frequently from the adjoining room accompanied by a lady friend. At one time Mrs. Lincoln exclaimed, sobbing bitterly: "Oh! that my little Taddy might see his father before he died!" This was decided not advisable. As Mrs. Lincoln sat on a chair by the side of the bed with her face to her husband's his breathing became very stertorous and the loud, unnatural noise frightened her in her exhausted, agonized condition. She sprang up suddenly with a piercing cry and fell fainting to the floor. Secretary Stanton hearing her cry came in from the adjoining room and with raised arms called out loudly: "Take that woman out and do not let her in again." Mrs. Lincoln was helped up kindly and assisted in a fainting condition from the room. Secretary Stanton's order was obeyed and Mrs. Lincoln did not see her husband again before he died.

As Captain Lincoln was consoling his mother in another room, and as I had promised Mrs. Lincoln to do all I possibly could for her husband, I took the place of kindred and continuously held the President's right hand firmly, with one exception of less than a minute, when my sympathies compelled me to seek the disconsolate wife. I found her reclining in a nearby room, being comforted by her son. Without stopping in my walk, I passed the room where Secretary Stanton sat at his official table and returning took the hand of the dying President in mine. The hand that had signed the Emancipation Proclamation liberating 4,000,000 slaves.

As morning dawned it became quite evident that the President was sinking, and at several times his pulse could not be counted. Two or three feeble pulsations being noticed, followed by an intermission when not the slightest movements of the artery could be felt. The inspirations became very prolonged and labored, accompanied by a guttural sound. The respirations ceased for some time and several anxiously looked at their watches until the profound silence was disturbed by a prolonged inspiration, which was followed by a sonorous expiration.

During these moments the Surgeon General occupied a chair by the head of the President's bed and occasionally held his finger over the carotid artery to note its pulsations. Dr. Stone sat on the edge of the foot of the bed, and I stood holding the President's right hand with my extended forefinger on his pulse, being the only one between the bed and the wall, the bed having been drawn out diagonally for that purpose. While we were anxiously watching in profound solemn silence, the Rev. Dr. Gurley said: "Let us pray," and offered a most impressive prayer. After which we witnessed the last struggle between life and death.

At this time my knowledge of physiology, pathology and psychology told me that the President was totally blind as a result of blood pressure on the brain, as indicated by the paralysis, dilated pupils, protruding and bloodshot eyes, but all the time I acted on the belief that if his sense of hearing or feeling remained, he could possibly hear me when I sent for his son, the voice of his wife when she spoke to him and that the last sound he heard, may have been his pastor's prayer, as he finally committed his soul to God.

Knowledge that frequently just before departure recognition and reason return to those who have been unconscious caused me for several hours to hold his right hand firmly within my grasp to let him in his blindness know, if possible, that he was in touch with humanity and had a friend.

The protracted struggle ceased at twenty minutes past seven o'clock on the morning of April 15, 1865, and I announced that the President was dead.

Immediately after death the few remaining in the room knelt around the bed while the Rev. Dr. Gurley delivered one of the most impressive prayers ever uttered, that our Heavenly Father look down in pity upon the bereaved family and preserve our afflicted and sorrow-stricken country.

Then I gently smoothed the President's contracted facial muscles, took two coins from my pocket, placed them over his eyelids and drew a white sheet over the martyr's face. I had been the means, in God's hand, of prolonging the life of President Abraham Lincoln for nine hours.

Every necessary act of love, devotion, skill and loyalty had been rendered during his helpless hours to the President of the United States, the Commander-in-Chief of the Army and Navy, to the beloved of millions of people throughout the world.

Many reported, anxious in any way to be of service. I accepted their offers to the extent of abundantly filling every want. Of all the people I have met in different parts of the world, I have found that as a class, good Americans are not to be excelled when occasions demand, in strength, endurance, calmness, good judgment, ardent loyal devotion and self-sacrificing love.

By prolonging the life of President Lincoln, his son Robert, whom I sent for, was enabled to see his father alive. Physicians and surgeons, lawyer and clergyman, whom I sent for, visited the President and were given time to deliberate. Members of the Cabinet, whom I sent for with soldiers and sailors and friends, had the opportunity to surround him. Millions of dangerous, excited and disappointed people were morally dissuaded from acts of discord. The nation was held in suppressed, sympathetic suspense and control, when the people heard that the President was living, though severely wounded and dying.

Before the people had time to realize the situation there was another President of the United States and the grandeur of the continuity of the Republic was confirmed.

After all was over, and as I stood by the side of the covered mortal remains I thought: "You have fulfilled your promise to the wife, your duty now is to the many living, suffering, wounded officers committed to your care in your ward at Armory Square General Hospital, and I left the house in deep meditation. In my lonely walk I was aroused from my reveries by the cold drizzling rain dropping on my bare head, my hat I had left in my seat at the theatre. My clothing was stained with blood, I had not once been seated since I first sprang to the President's aid; I was cold, weary and sad. The dawn of peace was again clouded, the most cruel war in history had not completely ended. Our long sorrowing country vividly came before me as I thought how essential it was to have an organization composed of returning soldiers to guard and protect the officers of state and uphold the Constitution. This great need was simultaneously recognized by others, for on that day, April 15, 1865, there assembled at Philadelphia a few army officers for that purpose and originated the Military Order of the Loyal Legion of the United States.

Among the archives of our organization, the Military Order of the Loyal Legion of the United States, we have recorded:—

ABRAHAM LINCOLN.

President of the United States, March 4, 1861, *to April* 15, 1865.
Born February 12, 1809, *Hardin (La Rue County), Kentucky.*
Assassinated April 14, 1865; *died April* 15, 1865, *at Washington, D.C.*
Enrolled by Special Resolution, to date from April 15, 1865.

I herewith give in the order in which they arrived, the names of the physicians and surgeons, and the clergyman whom I recognized as taking a professional part in the physical, mental or spiritual welfare of the President from the time he was shot until his death. The first person to enter the box after the President was shot, and who took charge of him at the request of Mrs. Lincoln, was myself, Charles A. Leale, M. D., Assistant Surgeon, United States Volunteers and the surgeon in charge of the ward containing the wounded commissioned officers at the United States Army General Hospital, Armory Square, Washington, D. C. The next who reported and simultaneously offered their services to me, which were accepted, were Charles S. Taft, M. D., Acting Assistant Surgeon, United States Army, and Albert F. A. King, M. D., Acting Assistant Surgeon, United States Army. Then apparently a very long time after we had cared for the President in Mr. Petersen's house, and in response to the numerous messengers whom I had sent, there arrived Robert K. Stone, M. D., Mrs. Lincoln's family physician; Joseph K. Barnes, M. D., Surgeon General, United States Army; Charles H. Crane, M. D., Assistant Surgeon General, United States Army, and the Rev. Dr. Gurley, Mrs. Lincoln's pastor. During the night several other physicians unknown to me called, and through courtesy I permitted some of them to feel the President's pulse, but none of them touched the wound.

Later in the forenoon as I was in the midst of important surgical duties at our hospital, I was notified by my lady nurse that a messenger had called inviting me to be present at the necropsy. Later a doctor called for the same purpose. I respectfully asked to be excused, as I did not dare to leave the large number of severely wounded expecting my usual personal care. I was fearful that the shock of hearing of the sudden death of the President might cause trouble in their depressed painful conditions.

One of my patients was profoundly depressed. He said to me: "Doctor, all we have fought for is gone. Our country is destroyed, and I want to die." This officer the day before was safely recovering from an amputation. I called my lady nurse, "Please closely watch Lieutenant ——; cheer him as much as possible, and give him two ounces of wine every two hours," etc., etc. This brave soldier received the greatest kindness and skillful care, but he would not rally from the shock and died in a short time.

Among my relics I have a photograph taken a few days later in full staff uniform as I appeared at the obsequies. The crape has never been removed from my sword. I have my cuffs stained with the martyr's blood, also my card of invitation to the funeral services, held on Wednesday, April 19, which I attended, having been assigned a place at the head of the coffin at the White House, and a carriage immediately preceding the catafalque in the grand funeral procession from the

White House to the Capitol; where during the public ceremonies I was assigned to a place at the head of the casket as it rested beneath the rotunda.

One of the most devoted of those who remained in the room with the dying President was Senator Charles Sumner, of Massachusetts. He visited me subsequently and said: "Dr. Leale, do you remember that I remained all the time until President Lincoln died?" Senator Sumner was profoundly affected by this great calamity to both North and South.

On my visit to Secretary Seward some time after the President's death, he was still suffering from his fracture and from the brutal attacks of the assassin, who made such a desperate attempt to kill him on that fatal night.

When I again met Secretary Stanton we sat alone in his private office. He was doing his utmost to continue what he deemed best for our country. The long continued strain and great burden had left their deep impress upon him. At the close of my call we shook hands fraternally.

After the war had closed Governor Fenton, of New York State, one of the "War Governors," came to me and said: "Dr. Leale, I will give you anything possible within my power." I responded: "I sincerely thank you, Governor; but I desire nothing, as I wish to follow my mission in life."

The city of Washington was wrapped in a mantle of gloom. The President had known his people and had a heart full of love for his soldiers and sailors. With "malice toward none" he alone seemed to have the power to restore fraternal love. He alone appeared able to quickly heal his country's wound.

In May there occurred in Washington one of the most pathetic and historic events, the return of the Northern Army for the final review of more than 70,000 veterans. A grandstand had been erected in front of the White House for the new President, his Cabinet, Officers of State, Foreign Ministers and others. I had a seat on this grandstand, from which on May 24th we watched one of the most imposing parades recorded in history. Among the many heroes, I recall the passing of stately General William Tecumseh Sherman on his majestic horse, which had been garlanded with roses. After we had been sitting there for several hours a foreign official tapped me on the shoulder and said: "What will become of these thousands of soldiers after their discharge?" I answered: "They will return to their homes all over the country and soon be at work doing their utmost to pay off the national debt." He replied: "Is it possible! No other country could expect such a result."

All had lost comrades, many were to return to desolate and broken homes. Amidst all the grandeur of victory there was profound sorrow. Among the thousands of passing veterans, there were many who looked for their former Commander-in-Chief, but their "Father Abraham" had answered to his last bugle call and with more than 300,000 comrades had been mustered out.